P9-DMH-067

REGIONS OF THE U.S.A.

The Southwest

by Rebecca Felix

PUBLISHED BY THE CHILD'S WORLD®

The Child's World®

Published by The Child's World®
1980 Lookout Drive • Mankato, MN 56003-1705
800-599-READ • www.childsworld.com

Acknowledgments
The Child's World®: Mary Berendes, Publishing Director
Red Line Editorial: Editorial direction
The Design Lab: Design
Amnet: Production
Design Elements: Dreamstime

Photographs ©: Photodisc, title, 3; Creatas, title, 3, 21; Comstock/Thinkstock, 3; iStockphoto/Thinkstock, title, 7, 12, 13, 16, 19, 23; Anton Foltin/Shutterstock Images, 4; Red Line Editorial, Inc., 5, 6; Jupiterimages/Thinkstock, 8; GSPhotography/Shutterstock Images, 9, 28; William Silver/Shutterstock Images, 11; Hemera/Thinkstock, 15; Brandon Seidel/Shutterstock Images, 17; Douglas Knight/Shutterstock Images, 18, 22; Medioimages/Photodisc/Thinkstock, 20; Diane Garcia/Shutterstock Images, 24, 31; Lori Martin/Shutterstock Images, 25; Brand X Images, 26, 27; Ken Durden/Shutterstock Images, 29

Front cover: iStockphoto/Thinkstock; Photodisc; Creatas; Comstock/Thinkstock

ISBN: 978-1623234942
LCCN: 2013931432

Printed in the United States of America
Mankato, MN
July, 2013
PA02170

ABOUT THE AUTHOR

Rebecca Felix is a writer and editor who grew up in the Midwest. She received a bachelor's degree in English from the University of Minnesota, which is her home state. She has edited and written several children's books and currently lives in Florida, which is in the Southeastern region of the United States.

Table of Contents

CHAPTER ONE

Canyons, Cacti, and Coyotes

Deep orange and red canyons sink into wide valleys. Coyotes and tumbleweeds cross deserts spotted with cacti. And miles of dry prairie turn to marsh and ocean coast. This U.S. region is called the Southwest. It is made up of four states. They are Arizona, New Mexico, Texas, and Oklahoma. Mexico and the Gulf of Mexico make up the southern border. U.S. states make up the remaining borders.

Much of the Southwest is made up of desert and canyon.

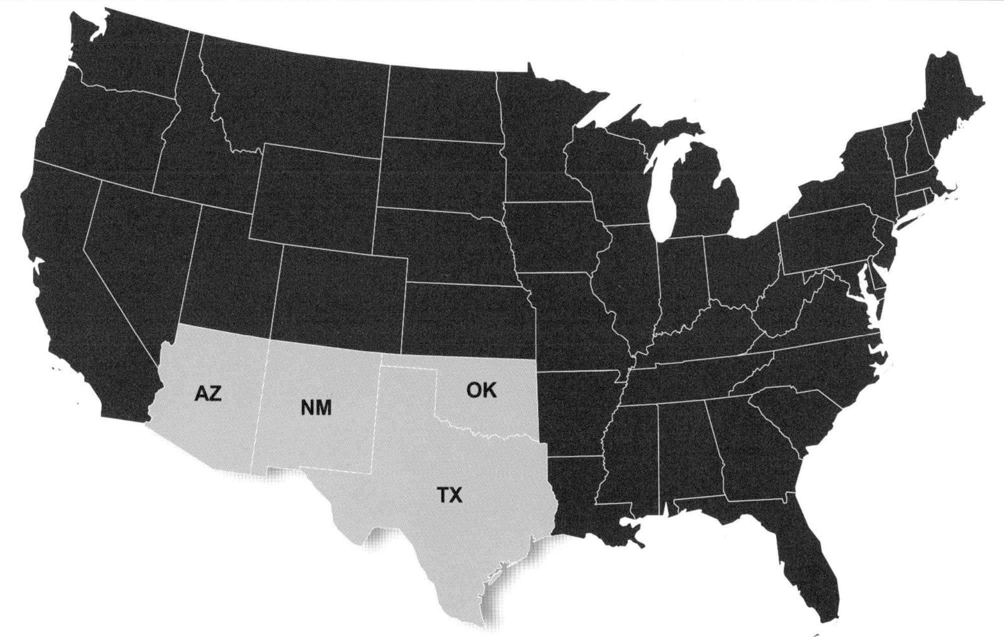

New Mexico, Arizona, Utah, and Colorado meet in one spot. This spot is called "Four Corners." It is the only place where four states meet in the United States.

Geography

There are many **geographic** features in the Southwest. The Coastal Plains are in southeast Texas. The land here is mainly flat. Some of the land is marsh. Marsh is a type of wetland. The rolling land of Texas is called Hill Country. It turns into the Great Plains in the north. Oklahoma is also in the Great Plains. The land here is mainly low prairie.

There are small mountain ranges throughout the Southwest. The Wichita Mountains and the Ozark

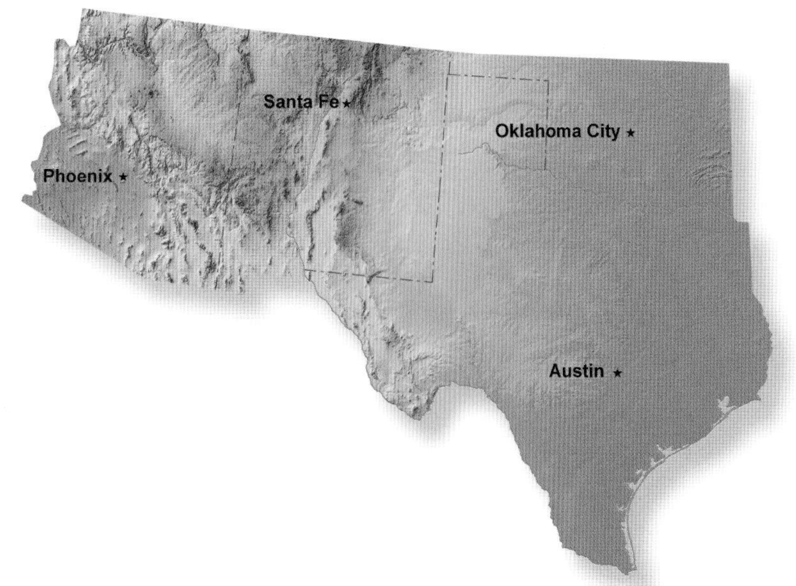

The Grand Canyon is 277 miles (446 km) long. It is 18 miles (29 km) wide in one spot. And it is more than one mile (1.6 km) deep in another!

Mountains are in Oklahoma. New Mexico's ranges include the Jemez Mountains. The White Mountains are in Arizona. The Davis Mountains are one of many ranges in Texas. Parts of the Rocky Mountains are also in the Southwest. It is the largest mountain range in North America. Part of this range is found in northern Arizona.

West of the Rocky Mountains is the Colorado Plateau. Land here is high and full of rock formations. The Colorado River has run through the plateau for thousands of years.

The Rocky Mountains block moisture from the Southwest.

This wore down the rock to create canyons. The Grand Canyon was also made this way. It is a major U.S. landmark in Arizona.

The Rio Grande flows along the southwest border of Texas. It also runs through Arizona. The Rio Grande splits along the Texas border. It branches to become the Pecos River.

Parts of the Sonoran Desert and Mojave Desert are in Arizona. Many types of cacti grow here. Cacti do not need much water to survive.

Climate

Most of the Southwest has arid, or dry, air. It is the driest U.S. region. Summers are very hot in the Southwest. Winters are usually very mild in Arizona and Texas. But winter temperatures can reach below freezing at night.

Warm or hot weather is most common in this region. Mountains also affect the climate. It is dry and hot because the mountains block moisture from the Pacific coast.

Not getting much rain makes the climate even hotter. It can also lead to **droughts**. Droughts in the Southwest can last for many years. They can also cause dust storms and wildfires. The Texas and Oklahoma panhandles make up part of the Dust Bowl. This is an area that experienced a long drought in the 1930s.

When it does rain in the Southwest, it can cause floods. This is because the rivers are wide and flat. They can quickly become overfilled. Tornadoes and hurricanes are also a threat in Texas and Oklahoma.

Texas experienced a seven-year drought during the 1950s.

The Gila monster is commonly seen in deserts of the Southwest.

Wildlife

The Southwest is home to many types of animals. There are deer, bighorn sheep, and mountain lions in Arizona

SOUTHWEST CAPITALS

The capital of Austin, Texas, is a unique city. "Keep Austin Weird" is its motto. It means the city likes to be different. Austin supports new and unusual musicians. Oklahoma City, Oklahoma, has a motto, too. It is *Labor omnia vincit*. This means "Labor Conquers All Things" in Latin. New Mexico's capital is Santa Fe. It means "Holy Faith" in Spanish. Phoenix, Arizona, also has a spiritual name. It is named after the phoenix, a mythical bird. A phoenix burned and then came alive from its ashes. The city of Phoenix was in ruins when it was found. Settlers believed a new city would rise from these ashes.

and New Mexico. Mountain lions live in Texas, too. Bison can be seen in Oklahoma. Coyotes live across the region. Reptiles in the Southwest include rattlesnakes and Gila monsters. Alligators live in Texas wetlands and rivers near the Gulf of Mexico coast.

Mountain lions are called many names. These include cougar, puma, and panther.

CHAPTER TWO

Native Tribes, Spanish Territory, and Trail of Tears

Before the 1500s there were many Native American tribes in the Southwest. Native American tribes of the Southwest included members of many Pueblo tribes. The Hopi, Apache, and Zuni were some Pueblo tribes. They consisted of many small tribes in Arizona, New Mexico, and Texas. The Plains Apache lived in Oklahoma. The Comanche tribes controlled many areas across Texas.

Many ancient Southwest Native American tribes were basket weavers. Many tribes still weave baskets today.

Creation of Colonies

Spanish explorers came to the Southwest in the mid-1500s. The Southwest was controlled by Spain at the time. The explorers set up colonies. San Gabriel was the first colony. It was set up in present-day New Mexico. Setting up colonies was not always easy or peaceful. Many Southwest Native American tribes fought to keep the colonists out. But Spanish colonists fought their way in. They spread to Arizona in the 1700s.

Explorers from Spain who came to America were called *conquistadors*.

Villages built by Pueblo tribes are popular tourist destinations.

European colonists were settling other areas of North America during this time. There was a war on the East Coast in the late 1700s.

The Louisiana Purchase included land in the Southwest.

These colonies gained independence from Great Britain and became the United States.

East Coast colonists began to explore and move west. France controlled a large portion of land west of the Mississippi River. The United States bought this land from France in 1803. This was called the Louisiana Purchase. It included northern parts of Texas and New Mexico. It also included all of Oklahoma. Colonists began moving to the Southwest in the early 1800s.

Davy Crockett was a famous American frontiersman. He was also a leader in the battle at the Alamo. He fought for Texas against Mexico.

Mexico lost one-third of its land in the Mexican-American War.

The United States passed the Indian Removal Act in 1830. It forced Native Americans east of the Mississippi River off their settled land. They had to move to unsettled lands in the West. These lands were called reservations. The Cherokee was one tribe forced to move to Oklahoma. They walked many miles to get there. This long path is called the Trail of Tears.

The Alamo was the site of a major battle in the fight for independence from Mexico.

Wars

In the early 1800s, Mexico fought for and won independence from Spain. Then people living in Texas fought for independence from Mexico. A major battle happened at the Alamo in San Antonio in 1836. Texas became an independent area for ten years. In 1845, Texas became a part of the United States. Mexico believed it still had control of some areas. The United States and Mexico did not agree on Texas's boundaries. This led to the Mexican-American War, which lasted four years. The United States gained areas of land from Mexico. This included the current states of Arizona, New Mexico, and Texas.

Southern and Northern states went to war in 1861. The two sides disagreed on slavery. Texas was a slave state. The Oklahoma territory also had slaves. Eleven states broke apart from the North. Texas was one of them. The war ended in 1865 and slavery was **abolished**. By 1912, all the Southwest states gained statehood. Texas became a state in 1845. Oklahoma followed in 1907. And Arizona and New Mexico became states in 1912.

Present Day

The Southwest is still home to many Native Americans. There is a large Navajo reservation in Arizona and New Mexico.

Arizona does not change times for daylight savings time. But the Navajo Nation does. So it is sometimes a different time on the reservation than in the rest of the state!

NAVAJO NATION

The largest reservation in the United States is the Navajo Nation. It was established in 1868. It covers more than 27,000 square miles (69,930 km). The reservation is in Arizona, New Mexico, and part of Utah. There are many national monuments within the reservation. Monument Valley is a large park with rock formations and red sandstone canyons. The Navajo people call themselves the *Diné*. The reservation has its own government. It is politically separate from the states it is in.

Many Hispanic people also still live in the Southwest. The history of the Southwest affects its government, **economy**, and culture.

CHAPTER THREE

Councils and Cattle

Window Rock, Arizona, is home to the Navajo Nation government.

States in the Southwest have three branches of government. Each state has an executive, a legislative, and a judicial branch. The Navajo Nation government also has three branches. Native American communities are partly under state and national law, too. The power a state government has over a reservation varies by tribe or state. It can also vary depending on any crime that occurs.

Texas has 254 counties. That is more than any other U.S. state.

The capitol building in Austin, Texas, houses all three branches of the state's government.

A governor is the head of a state's executive branch. A governor's job is to manage state policies and programs. Governors also oversee state laws. The head of the Navajo Nation executive branch is the president. The Navajo president is voted into office for four years.

Window Rock, Arizona, is the capital of the Navajo Nation. The reservation's government meets there.

State legislatures write laws in the legislative branch. They also make sure state budgets are on track. Two groups, or chambers, do these jobs in each state. Dividing duties keeps power in balance. The Navajo Nation also has a legislative branch. It is called the Navajo Nation Council. The council makes the reservation laws.

State judicial branches are made up of the state's court systems. The Navajo Nation has its own court system, too. It handles cases for the reservation's 11 districts.

Texas Longhorn is a type of Southwest cattle. Males have long horns that turn up at the ends.

Economy

Much of the land in the Southwest is dry with little rain. This can make agriculture difficult. Droughts and dust storms damage crops, which can hurt the economy. For this reason, irrigation is important in

There are a lot of cattle ranches in the Southwest.

One area of the Rio Grande Valley in Texas has a very long growing season. It is more than 280 days a year.

the Southwest. Irrigation is using something other than rain to water crops. The Southwest climate benefits agriculture, too. It provides a longer growing season. Crops produced in the Southwest include cotton, citrus, and alfalfa. Alfalfa is often used to feed cattle. And there are a lot of cattle in the Southwest!

They are raised on ranches. Beef is a major **export** of Oklahoma, Texas, and Arizona. Texas is the top beef producer in the country.

Industry is also important in the Southwest. Oil is a major industry in Oklahoma, Texas, and New Mexico. Texas is again a leader in this area. Oklahoma is also a major producer of natural

One of the major industries in the Southwest is oil.

gas. Copper mining is a large industry in Arizona and New Mexico. Manufacturing of space exploration equipment is big in Oklahoma.

The Southwest climate attracts many visitors. Some come for health reasons. The dry, clear air is good for people with breathing problems. Tourist attractions bring people to the Southwest, too. They come to see the Grand Canyon,

Most water in the Southwest used for irrigation comes from the Colorado River or the Rio Grande.

Monument Valley is another popular tourist attraction in the Southwest.

COWBOY TOURISM

Cowboy culture is present across the Southwest. Many people picture Southwest people rounding up cattle on a ranch, or at a rodeo riding a wild bull. People visit the Southwest to see and experience these things. Tourists can go on cattle drives. They can also visit rodeos or ride horse trails. Some horse trails go right through the Grand Canyon. Tourists can also visit the National Cowboy and Western Heritage Museum. It is in Oklahoma City. They can buy cowboy clothing in many places. Tourism from cowboy culture is important to the economy.

The first U.S. rodeo was in 1888. It was held in Prescott, Arizona. It still runs today.

Monument Valley, and many other landmarks. The money from tourism boosts the economy.

CHAPTER FOUR

Cultures, Big Cities, and Chiles

Hispanic artwork is seen throughout the region.

The Southwest is a region of many cultures and **ethnicities**. These include many Native Americans and Hispanic people. Native Americans make up most of the population in rural areas. There are also many people of European descent living in urban areas. The Coastal Plains in Texas are especially populated. Many Native Americans live in cities, as well.

More than 300,000 Native Americans live in Arizona and New Mexico.

Hispanic culture is very influential in the Southwest. Many towns have Spanish names. These include Santa Fe and El Paso in Texas, and Mesa, Arizona. Albuquerque, New Mexico, was named after a Spanish royal. Most people who live in New Mexico live near Albuquerque.

The Southwest is full of historic Spanish architecture. Hispanic cultures still influence the way of life in the area. This is because the Southwest was once part of Mexico. Many Mexicans move to the Southwest. Mexican food, music, and clothing are common in the region. And many people speak Spanish.

Historic Native American architecture is present in the Southwest, too. Buildings are called pueblos. More than 20 percent of the U.S. Native American

A pueblo is a common architectural style in the Southwest.

population lives in the Southwest. Their ways of life, art, clothing, and food are a part of Southwest culture. Southwest Native American traditions and culture are often celebrated at festivals.

Although rodeos are common in the Southwest, not everyone is a cowboy or cowgirl.

Ranch or cowboy culture also influences the way of life in the Southwest. Many people raise livestock on ranches. They also ride horses or participate in rodeos. Many people in the Southwest enjoy watching and listening to theater and musical performances. Football is popular in Texas. Many weekends in the fall are spent watching high school, college, and professional football.

Many people in Texas and Oklahoma have **accents** or a "drawl." They often draw words out slower than most people.

Many people think everything in Texas is big. They think Texans like big trucks, big jewelry, and big hats. This may be what some Texans like, but not everyone.

Texas is a big state, though. It also has many big cities. These include Houston, Dallas, and San Antonio. Each of these cities is home to more than one million people! Other big cities in the Southwest include Phoenix, Arizona, Oklahoma City, Oklahoma, and Albuquerque, New Mexico.

Food in the Southwest is influenced by the region's original cultures.

Football is an important part of Southwest culture, especially in Texas. Many people watch and go to games.

Food

The Southwest's original cultures influence the area's foods. Native American and Spanish foods are common. Many dishes have corn, chiles, tomatoes, and beans. Pork and beef are main ingredients in many

dishes, too. Two types of cuisine are very common in today's Southwest. They are called Tex-Mex and New Mexican-style. Tex-Mex uses ingredients from both Mexican and American dishes. Beef, melted cheese, and beans are common. Dishes are often served in tortillas. They usually have added spices for flavor. Fajitas are one example of a Tex-Mex dish. New Mexican-style dishes often have green chiles. There are many kinds of chiles used in Southwest cooking. They can be very hot. Barbeque is another common type of Southwest food. Dishes such as ribs and brisket are popular, especially in Texas and Oklahoma.

The many flavors and cultures of the Southwest make it a special place. Its history, climate, and people are unlike any other region.

More than 200 types of chiles are eaten in Southwest food.

Chiles are a common ingredient in dishes in the Southwest.

RECIPE

CHILE CON QUESO

Ingredients:

1/2 cup pre-chopped onions

4 ounce can diced green chiles

10 ounces chopped tomatoes

2 cups shredded Monterey jack cheese

2 cups shredded sharp cheddar cheese

1 bag tortilla chips

large microwaveable bowl

Directions:

Mix onions, chiles, tomatoes, and cheese in the microwaveable bowl. Leave the bowl uncovered. Microwave on high power for one to two minutes. Use a hot pad holder to take the bowl out of the microwave. Stir and then place in the microwave again. Cook for another one to two minutes on high power. Remove the bowl again. Check if the cheese is melted. If it is not, cook for one minute. Once cheese is melted, stir. Let the mixture cool for one or two minutes. Then dip tortilla chips in and enjoy!

Fast Facts

Population: 38,512,816 (2012 estimate)

Most populous state: Texas (26,059,203, 2012 estimate)

Least populous state: New Mexico (2,085,538, 2012 estimate)

Area: 574,066 square miles (1,486,824 sq km)

Highest temperature: 128 degrees Fahrenheit (53°C) in Arizona in 1994

Lowest temperature: minus-50 degrees Fahrenheit (-46°C), in New Mexico in 1951

Largest cities: Houston, Texas; Phoenix, Arizona; San Antonio, Texas; Dallas, Texas; Austin, Texas; Fort Worth, Texas

Major sports teams: Arizona Diamondbacks (MLB, baseball); Dallas Cowboys (NFL, football); Houston Texans (NFL, football); San Antonio Spurs (NBA, basketball); Texas Longhorns (college, football); Texas Rangers (MLB, baseball); Texas A&M Aggies (college, football)

Glossary

abolished (uh-BAH-lished) When a practice is officially ended, it is abolished. Slavery was abolished after the U.S. Civil War.

accents (AK-sents) Accents are the way people say the sounds that make up words. Some Southwest people have an accent that is called a drawl.

droughts (drouts) Droughts are long periods of time without rain. Southwest droughts can last for many years.

economy (i-KON-uh-mee) Economy is the system of making, buying, and selling things. The economy of the Southwest includes agriculture and business.

ethnicities (eth-NIH-sit-ees) Ethnicities are associations with certain groups of people of the same culture. Ethnicities of people in the Southwest include Native American and Hispanic.

export (EK-sport) An export is a product that is made in one place and sold to another place. Beef is an export of the Southwest.

geographic (jee-ah-GRAF-ic) An area's physical features, such as mountains and lakes, are geographic features. Canyons are a geographic feature of the Southwest.

industry (IN-duh-stree) An industry is a group of businesses. The oil industry is important to the economy in the Southwest.

To Learn More

Books

Peppas, Lynn. *What's in the Southwest?* New York: Crabtree, 2011.

Rau, Dana Meachen. *The Southwest*. New York: Scholastic, 2012.

Stone, Tanya Lee. *Regional Wild America: Unique Animals of the Southwest*. Detroit, MI: Blackbirch Press, 2005.

Web Sites

Visit our Web site for links about the Southwest:

childsworld.com/links

Note to Parents, Teachers, and Librarians:
We routinely verify our Web links to make sure they are safe and active sites. So encourage your readers to check them out!

Index